SONNETS
From Later Life

SONNETS
From Later Life
1981 - 1993

Kenneth E. Boulding

Pendle Hill Publications
Wallingford, Pennsylvania 19086

Printed in the United States of America
by Thomson-Shore, Inc., Dexter, Michigan

Book design by Eva Fernandez Beehler and Sage Publications
Cover art by Kenneth E. Boulding

The editor wishes to thank the following for their kind permission to reprint poems:

INTERNATIONAL INSTITUTE FOR APPLIED SYSTEMS ANALYSIS.
"Sonnets from Laxenburg: On the Numbers Zero to Ten" were written during a visit to the
IIASA System and Decision Sciences Area, June 20-July 2, 1981, and were published as a
pamphlet by IIASA, December, 1981; "Eleven" and "Twelve" were written after returning
home and were not published.

SOUTHEAST YEARLY MEETING.
"On Hearing of a Sudden Death," *SEYM Newsletter*, 23, i (Winter 1983): 3.

CENTER FOR CONFLICT RESOLUTION, GEORGE MASON UNIVERSITY.
"In the Washington National Arboretum," *Resolution*, 1, v (November 1985): 10.

UNIVERSITY OF COLORADO AT BOULDER.
"Sonnets for the Learning of Peace" (written at the Peace Studies 4th Annual Conference),
The Peace Studies Bulletin, 1, iii (Spring 1992): 1.

ASIAN PEACE RESEARCH ASSOCIATION.
"Sonnet for Peace," *Peace & Security in the Asia-Pacific Region: Cold War Problems and Prospects*
(Final Report of the Asian Peace Research Association Regional Conference, held at the
University of Canterbury, New Zealand, January 31-February 4, 1992), p. 5.

Library of Congress Cataloging-in-Publication Data
Boulding, Kenneth Ewart, 1910-1993
    Sonnets from later life, 1981–1993/Kenneth Ewart Boulding.

    ISBN 0-87574-920-8: $12.00
    1. Sonnets, American.   I. Title.
PS3503.0756S64   1994
811'.54--dc20   94-30016
                                             CIP

TABLE OF CONTENTS

PREFACE

Few publishers want to publish poetry. Poetry is not read; poetry does not sell. And of all forms of poetry, the most forbidding and therefore least likely to be read or to sell is the sonnet—so artificially restricted to its fourteen lines; so corseted within its strictness of rhyme, its division into octave and sestet (Petrarchan type) or into three quatrains and a gnomic final couplet (Elizabethan type, the one favored by Kenneth Boulding); so out of fashion in an era of experimentalism and free verse. Yet Pendle Hill dares to publish this volume of 146 sonnets. Why? Because they are a remarkable testimony not only to their author's spirit but also to the tradition that they revive and extend.

I want to consider that tradition first, before turning to the Boulding sonnets themselves. As a form, the sonnet began during the Italian Renaissance, the great practitioners being Petrarch, Dante, Tasso, and Michelangelo. The form followed the Renaissance to Portugal (Camoens), France (Marot), Spain (Boscán Almogaver), and England (Wyatt, Surrey, Spenser, Shakespeare, Milton). Then it languished for a time until it was cultivated again in the Romantic period by Goethe in Germany and Wordsworth and Keats in England. Elizabeth Barrett Browning wrote sonnets in the later nineteenth century, as did Longfellow. In the twentieth, although Auden, Yeats, and Frost continued to write some, T.S. Eliot wrote none. By and large, they were out of fashion in Kenneth Boulding's generation.

Non-specialists, if they have any acquaintance at all with sonnets, will most likely know the Shakespearean examples and therefore assume that the form is used primarily for love-poems ("Shall I compare thee to a summer's day? / Thou art more lovely and more temperate") or for meditations on the decline of beauty ("When forty winters shall besiege thy brow, / And dig deep trenches in thy beauty's field"). But the sonnet tradition houses subjects much more diverse. These include politics, death, poetry itself, bereavement and suffering, self-communing, self-justification. Milton's examples show this diversity and are the touchstone for all future sonnets, including Kenneth Boulding's. Here is the fierce opening quatrain of a sonnet written around 1645 after Milton had been attacked for his tracts against divorce:

> I did but prompt the age to quit their clogs
> By the known rules of ancient liberty,
> When straight a barbarous noise environs me
> Of owls and cuckoos, asses, apes and dogs.

And here, in quite a different mood, is Milton's 1655 lamentation on his blindness. He had lost his eyesight three years earlier at age 44 in preparing the Commonwealth's reply to *The Support of the King* by Salmasius. We need to remember, of course, that if he had never come to terms with this tragedy he would never have written *Paradise Lost*. Presumably part of the process of coming to terms was the writing of this sonnet. It is addressed to Cyriack Skinner.

> Cyriack, this three years' day these eyes, though clear
> To outward view of blemish or of spot,
> Bereft of light their seeing have forgot,
> Nor to their idle orbs doth sight appear
> Of sun or moon or star throughout the year,
> Or man or woman. Yet I argue not
> Against heaven's hand or will, nor bate a jot
> Of heart or hope; but still bear up and steer

Right onward. What supports me, dost thou ask?
The conscience, Friend, to have lost them overplyed
In liberty's defence, my noble task,
Of which all Europe talks from side to side.
This thought might lead me through the world's vain mask
Content though blind, had I no better guide.

Milton's combination of political grit and personal sensitivity endeared his sonnets to William Wordsworth a century and a half later, as we see in this celebrated example written in 1802 when Wordsworth was discouraged by England's selfish territorial and commercial designs:

Milton! thou shouldst be living at this hour:
England hath need of thee; she is a fen
Of stagnant waters: altar, sword, and pen,
Fireside, the heroic wealth of hall and bower,
Have forfeited their ancient English dower
Of inward happiness. We are selfish men;
Oh! raise us up, return to us again;
And give us manners, virtue, freedom, power.
Thy soul was like a Star, and dwelt apart:
Thou hadst a voice whose sound was like the sea:
Pure as the naked heavens, majestic, free,
So didst thou travel on life's common way,
In cheerful godliness; and yet thy heart
The lowliest duties on herself did lay.

To sum up this diverse tradition, perhaps the best way is to let Wordsworth speak again:

Scorn not the Sonnet; Critic, you have frowned,
Mindless of its just honours, with this key

Shakespeare unlocked his heart; the melody
Of this small lute gave ease to Petrarch's wound;
A thousand times this pipe did Tasso sound;
With it Camoens soothed an exile's grief;
The Sonnet glittered a gay myrtle leaf
Amid the cypress with which Dante crowned
His visionary brow: a glow-worm lamp,
It cheered mild Spenser, called from Faery-land
To struggle through dark ways; and, when a damp
Fell round the path of Milton, in his hand
The Thing became a trumpet; when he blew
Soul-animating strains—alas, too few!

This is what Kenneth Boulding inherited, revived, and extended. We certainly cannot chide him for composing too few sonnets! Quite aside from earlier ones (including *There is a Spirit: The Nayler Sonnets*, recently republished by Pendle Hill and Quaker Home Service) there are 216 written between 1981 and 1993, the period of this collection. Of these, as Elise Boulding tells us in her Introduction, 143 were composed in the thirteen months of his final illness, from January 1992 until February 1993, which means an average of one sonnet about every two and three-quarter days! What happened was that as advancing cancer sapped Boulding's energy to the point where lecturing, traveling, and the writing of books all had to be abandoned, the writing of sonnets became increasingly central to his life.

Requiring only short bursts of creative energy, they enabled him to unlock his heart; ease his wound, soothe his grief; cover with gay myrtle the cypresses of his despondency; travel back and forth between fairyland and the dark ways of hospital and sickroom; blow soul-animating strains; even recapture Shakespeare's sentiments of love—the entire Wordsworthian repertory, plus some.

The extensive range of Boulding's poems is indicated by the rubrics under which they have been arranged for this collection, starting with sonnets on sonnets themselves and on poetry as a whole; moving to meditations on science, nature, human nature, war and peace; then to considerations of social science in general and of his own career in particular; then to questions of faith, marriage, home, time's thievery; finally to aging, sickness, and death.

Earlier, I called these poems a remarkable testimony both to the tradition they revive and to their author's spirit. One reason is the extended range to which I have been referring. Another is their uniqueness. Who else has written a sonnet sequence on the numbers 1 through 12, indeed a sequence that requires not twelve but fifteen sonnets because one is devoted to Zero, another to "e" ("Along the road, somewhere 'twixt two and three"), and still another to "π" ("Nearly one-seventh of the way to four")? An additional reason is their humor, typically self-deprecating, never a cruel jibe at someone else's expense. Witness "Sonnet for My Morning Tub":

> . . . Immersion is a sacred rite
> Of spiritual power, so I've been told.
> If water is too hot, turn on the cold;
> If it's too cold, the hot tap makes it right.
> The Aristotelian Mean's clearly in sight
> And in our power! How wisdom can unfold!

We need to realize that by March 1992, the time of this poem, Kenneth Boulding was already extremely ill, Not too long afterward, merely getting in and out of the tub became a major accomplishment. Even earlier, when his cancer was not yet declared and he was suffering only the relatively minor annoyances of old age,

Boulding had learned to cope *by observing*. We see this, for example, in "Sonnet for My Stiff Knees":

> The human body is a work of art,
> . . . .
> It's like a horse, too, pulling a complex cart
> But sometimes, traveling in a rough domain,
> The parts rebel, and though with might and main
> The horse pulls, still the wheels refuse to start.

In October 1992, when cancer was diagnosed and he was given perhaps six months to live, he felt paradoxically relieved because at last he knew the truth. He resolved to make the best of his remaining time. Given the physical disabilities that sapped his strength and limited his movements, this meant, even more than before, the imperative need to *observe*. The very next First Day he ministered in Meeting for Worship about how in his youth, in Quaker meeting, he had experienced what living in the Eternal Now meant, and how that experience was returning to him at present. Immediately afterwards, Elise Boulding recorded in her diary, "My fear that he wouldn't be able to use this time for spiritual growth has vanished." Later, in February 1993, while in hospital after breaking his hip, he said to Elise with a smile, "Death is a wonderful invention—everyone should try it."

In all this he reminds us of Virginia Woolf, who wrote in her diary on March 8, 1941, three weeks before her death: "I mark Henry James's sentence: Observe perpetually. Observe the oncome of age. Observe greed. Observe my own despondency. . . . I insist upon spending this time to the best advantage. I will go down with my colours flying. . . ."

Pendle Hill is publishing these sonnets even though poetry

does not sell and even though this particular poetic form is un-fashionable, perhaps forbidding. Why are we doing this? Because these sonnets continue the soul-animating strains of the form's re-markable tradition and because they demonstrate so memorably that if one uses everything for spiritual growth—even aging, dis-ability, time's thievery, the refusal of the wheels to start, death it-self—turning all these negatives into opportunities, one will in-deed go down, like Kenneth Boulding, with colors flying.

Peter Bien
Publications Committee

INTRODUCTION

Nobody ever loved life more than Kenneth Boulding. Not long before he went into his final coma, he smiled and said, "I love the world." It is not surprising, then, that he did not make a big deal of solemn spiritual preparations for dying. But a few weeks before his death he grinned at me one morning and said, "I know this sounds ridiculous, but I feel like having a baby!" I grinned back. He was getting ready to give birth to life after life.

At another level, Kenneth's Other Lifetime Companion, his Muse, initiated certain processes somewhere deep inside that extraordinarily vivid and capacious mind that made Kenneth the unique scientist-poet-godseeker-worldlover he was. The hints of those processes come out most clearly in the sonnets that in my own mind I think of as his "On Pilgrimage" sonnets. Already in 1983 we hear Kenneth saying, "And when the doors fling wide I will be ready." To the end, Kenneth experienced both poetry and music as an inward joy that made him want to dance. Our last stately two-step, performed together when walking had already become very difficult for him, was danced to the sound of our son Philip's harp.

Kenneth's love of home and the daily round was the magical golden thread that kept us connected through his many travels to far places. I can still hear his voice in my mind, calling out joyfully, "I'm home!" to the sound of the opening of the front door. The absence might have been a day or a month, but the delight in homecoming was always fresh and new. In the last nine months, when Kenneth was wheelchair bound and his physical world had shrunk to the four walls of the apartment and the immediate neighborhood, his love of every detail of our apartment and balcony, of the nearby Creek path and mall, grew ever deeper. This love gives the sonnets about Home a special poignancy.

There was a steady crescendo of sonnets in his later years, particularly in the last year and a half. He wrote 143 sonnets from January 3, 1992 to February 6, 1993, and left three unfinished sonnets in his last weeks. The Muse usually woke him around 4 AM, and it was one of our special family jokes that I never minded his fidelity to that lady, the Muse, who regularly slept between us. In the last year, I made sure there was always pen and paper at his bedside each evening.

As Kenneth neared the great transition, we both found little need for talking. I sat by his bed and sang to him the hymns he had taught me when we were first married, hymns we had so happily sung together in our own special duet over the years. Mostly there was a silent dialogue of loving looks and gestures. But the Muse and he worked the journey out in their own way, and I was kept attuned through the sonnets that continued to flow. The sonnet "Outrageous Joy" captures most perfectly the spirit in which he entered his next life:

> Absurd joy to the world, the Lord is come
> Like fresh sap rising in a withered tree
> A flame of praise, rising exultantly
> Beyond all reason in a world so glum.
> There is a vast refreshment in the sky—
> What matters cliffs indeed to those who fly!

Elise Boulding

ON SONNETS

SONNET FOR SONNETS

24 January 1992

To crush a crowd of words into a sonnet
May need to be defended when it's done.
A narrow room does not afflict a nun,
However tight the armor, knights will don it.
When tangled hair is pushed into a bonnet,
Beauty may be enhanced—and so may fun.
Raindrops will make a rainbow from the sun,
And who will buy what has no label on it?

Poets today are liberated—free
From rhythm, rhyme, and structure—even sense,
Producing with their freedom an immense
Fog of unreadable obscurity.
    So, at risk of seeming orthodox
    I'll squeeze my words into the sonnet's box.

(With apologies to Wordsworth's "Nuns fret not at their convent's narrow room.")

IN DEFENSE OF SONNETS
11 May 1992

To push good words into a sonnet's packet,
May seem like "the unkindest cut of all,"*
But people jammed into a concert hall
Are there to hear tight music, not a racket.
Uncontrollables need a strait jacket,
Riots delete shops from a shopping mall.
Only tight ships survive a violent squall;
When garbage overflows we have to sack it.

The body is confined within its skin,
The mind within an even smaller skull,
Good gardeners must trim and weed and cull,
And even food keeps better in a tin!
    Poets may scold—but I won't hesitate
    My sonnets to pursue—and celebrate!

*(*Shakespeare, Julius Caesar, III . ii. 188)*

SONNET FOR MY MUSE

15 December 1991

I

My Muse, hid in a cavern in my mind,
Seems inexhaustibly to feed
Upon the many sonnets that I read,
And then in lightning searches she can find
Among the words that to my memory bind
Just those that meet her sharp, controlling need,
In what seems like almost linguistic greed,
And links each one to its true mate assigned.

And then—from deep within the viewless cave
Come words, into my mind and to my pen;
Another sonnet springs to life again,
Splashing upon my paper like a wave.
    I feel her, always making things anew,
    Yet never, never, coming into view.

SONNET FOR MY MUSE

19 January 1992

II

Oh, why, my muse, are you so busy now
In your secluded corner of my brain?
For every night you seem to strike again
Behind my very slightly furrowed brow.
You search my language bank, I know not how,
And fish out words, and rhymes, in a long train
From where they have so comfortably lain,
And trail long sentences behind your plow.

The words you pull out wrap themselves around
The skeletons of one or two ideas,
And then to my astonishment appears
A sonnet more—or sometimes less—profound.
　　For this, of course, I have to thank you, Muse,
　　But is it you, or is it I, who choose?

BIRTH OF A SONNET
FOR MY 83rd BIRTHDAY
15-18 January 1993

The Muse says she has a sonnet coming,
Though where's the charm in number 83?
Still, if the Muse decides to have a spree,
I wouldn't want to interrupt her chumming.
She can occasionally be quite numbing,
But if she pesters me, I should feel free
To do what she commands. The words i see
Will creep into a pattern that's becoming.

I see a something that could be a verse,
A structure that with ten beats will conform
Into a rhyme and rhythm with a norm
At least historic, patterned, close and tense;
    Then if the muse will gently breathe upon it,
    It will turn into something like this sonnet.

SONNET FOR A RELUCTANT MUSE

March 1992

Sometimes a sonnet can't get itself written,
When some essential word lacks enough rhymes,
And so there come somewhat distressful times,
When we just can't find words to try our wit on.
A thought that is as playful as a kitten
And rings poetic bells with a loud chime,
May turn out to be worthless as a dime,
Because there are no rhymes that it can sit on.

So, throw the frustrated sonnet lines away,
Unless from the reluctant muse we borrow
Time to reveal an unfound rhyme tomorrow,
That just eludes our frantic search today.
    Or—our frustration we will bravely bear,
    Knowing we cannot find what isn't there.

SILLY SONNET

9 February 1992

Where do you fall to when you fall asleep?
How wide are you when you are wide awake?
Where does thirst go to when your thirst you slake?
How deep is what stuff when your thought is deep?
Just how much dust is piled up in a heap?
What are you making when your way you make?
What is it taking when it takes the cake?
What do you sow when what you sow you reap?

What then is language but a bunch of words
Strung altogether by a sort of string
That doesn't really have to say a thing?
Milk, after all, can make delicious curds,
    And where there's not a shadow of pretense
    Nonsense can make just as much sense as sense.

SLIGHTLY AGAINST RULES

22 February 1992

Sonnets confine themselves with rhythm and rhyme,
As Science also does with Mathematics.
But somewhere, in the mind's extensive attics,
Are leftovers from an earlier time,
And so it can't be counted as a crime
To do a little mental acrobatics
And bend the rhyming with a bit of tactics,
And temper mathematics with a mime.

For things that are alike are not the same,
No law is made that can't somewhere be broken.
Brooklyn, indeed, can never be Hoboken,
And we can halt without becoming lame.
    Each thing's unique. Nothing can really fit.
    And every "x" smells of the infinite.

THE MUSE

August 1992

"Muse, tell me you have not gone away
For still you have some powerful truths to find,
You are so much at home within my mind
There's no way I can bid you a 'good day.'
Do not abandon me, I therefore pray,
We still have verse and meter to unwind
From the great spool of language—still, still bind
Your powers to mine, in fruitful interplay."

"Don't worry, Friend, you made me by your learning,
Without you I would not be here at all.
Your learning does not cease—or even stall.
Our cells are common, as you are discerning.
    Even if I were a figment of your mind,
    There's no way known by which we could unbind."

SONNETINA FOR RHYME AND METER
15 April 1992

I'm moved to sing the praise of rhyme,
That modern poets rudely spurn;
It is not very hard to learn,
Although it takes a little time.
For surely it is not a crime
To search the mind for words that turn
Toward each other, to discern
An echo that can make them chime.

Then also, let's give praise to meter,
For surely it cannot be wrong
To have a poem echo song,
And rhythm always makes words sweeter.
    And if no rhyme or meter's on it,
    Well! what would happen to the sonnet?

ON POETRY, POETS, AND MUSIC

LANGUAGE AS MIRACLE
November 1992

Amazing! how the half-awakened mind
Can turn experience into memory.
Experience has form but cannot see
Unless changed into language that can find
Form in speech, writing, words that are designed
To pattern the experience accurately
In other minds experimentally,
In words that somehow with clear meanings bind.

How can word-patterns from no pattern grow
That reproduce in other minds the experience
Of one—extracting from the common sense
A common truth that everywhere will show?
    It seems to be a fact empirical
    That language is an endless miracle.

SONNET FOR DANGEROUS POETRY
3 March 1992

Poetry is dangerous. It can blow the lock
On the odiferous closets of the mind,
And, when these doors are open, what we find
May break all fences down, put us in shock.
Privacy is destroyed, and earthquakes rock
The castles and the temples we designed
To keep things orderly, and great mills grind
To powder all defenses kept in stock.

Yet poetry has its own rebuilding powers.
Its ancient forms of order reassert
The skills to build new cities out of dirt,
And make old seeds burst into novel flowers.
    So let's not be afraid. Rhythm and rhyme
    Will help us bear even the truth, in time.

ON READING
SHAKESPEARE'S SONNETS
30 July 1992

Words, in their cadences, sound in my ears
With endless music—all that language bears
Though sometimes distant discords will appear,
As when we find love's fears and pains and cares.
That echo in the caverns of the mind
The universe of love's woes and delights
Spreads out before us like a map we find
Seen from imagination's highest flights.

How did a man from a small country town,
Not even of an intellectual class,
Achieve such wisdom, knowledge, and renown?
We cannot know how such things come to pass,
    But in the presence of so great a voice
    All that we need to know is to rejoice.

Kyoto, Japan

SONNET FOR JOHN DONNE

14 May 1992

Like a great tolling bell, your words, John Donne,
Boom in my ear, like an enormous gong.
Confessing agonizing sin and wrong,
Shoot in my mind like an enormous gun.
You do to words what had never been done;
Quite ruthlessly, you carry them along
To deepest Hell, where they are stripped of song,
Of joy, peace, dignity, of simple fun.

But then, with words too, you will bring the Christ,
The Word, to bear you from the deepest flame
That any mind can reach, or word can name.
But then, Ah! then, by nothing more enticed
 Than pure repentance, all this washed away,
 And we are in the world of every day.

ON READING WORDSWORTH
BEFORE GOING TO SLEEP
15 November 1990

Wordsworth! Across the centuries and the miles
You speak to me, in language like the rill
That flowed so eloquently down the hill,
In liquid pleasure laced with quiet smiles.
Here are no great processions down the aisles
Of vast cathedrals, but a gentle, still
Harmony of an earth-surrendered will,
Untainted by prim artifice or wiles.

Sometimes the verse almost embraces prose,
Long cadences, expressing inward trains
Of long remembered joys and present pains,
Tell of the peace that over all things rose.
    Distance in time and space become absurd,
    For I am one with you in thought and word.

SONNET FOR ALFRED, LORD TENNYSON

31 March 1992

Across the many miles and years that separate
Our bodies, my mind reaches out to yours,
In poetry, the passion that outpours
From the experience of loss, of fate,
Of Nature, that seems to deny the great
Omnipotence of Love: the festering sores
Of unforgiveness, and the doubt that bores
Through the great temple that our hopes create.

You say, "Are God and Nature then at strife?"*
In the great patterned web of time and space
Unless there's bright and dark, we could not trace
The subtle clues that give meaning to life
    And death, the good, the ill, reward, and cost.
    With nothing but pure light, design is lost.

(*In Memoriam, LV)

SONNET FOR MUSIC
25 April 1992

Music is very different from speech:
It asks no question and requires no answer
It's useful—for the singer and the dancer—
But in its pure form it will never preach.
It sometimes is a little out of reach,
Sometimes it shoots a message like a lancer,
It's far too orderly to be a cancer,
It never has to wheedle or beseech.

All that it gives us is ongoing pleasure,
Without hidden agendas, shame, or guilt
Toward which so many other pleasures tilt.
It is indeed the purest of all treasures.
    It asks no favors, it demands no duty,
    For all it has to offer us is beauty.

While listening to the Takacs Quartet perform, Boulder, Colorado.

SONNET FOR THE TRINITY OF MUSIC
8 June 1992

Music is strangely like a trinity!
Music the Father is the basic laws
That govern sounds and brain, and give them cause
To realize their strange affinity.
Music the Son brings down the infinity
To human earth. Composers may have flaws,
But Handel, Bach, by opening Music's doors
Bring to the earth hints of Divinity.

The Holy Spirit is the one who plays
The music captured by the father's sons
So that in our own ears the music runs,
Interpreted in many different ways.
    And yet we cannot find true Unity,
      Unless the three are one, the one is three.

SONNET FOR THE HARP
9 May 1992

A precious gift to music is the harp;
Its form is graceful as a dancer's pose,
With gentle curves and string in ordered rows,
It does much more than sing—its notes are sharp,
The fingers climb up high upon a scarp,
And then glissando down into repose.
The mind in hearing it not only glows,
But leaps out of its torpor, as a carp

Leaps from its pond. And when it plays with strings
In concert, music new dimensions takes,
Uniting continuities with breaks
The mellow with the sharp, a whole, that brings
    To the awaiting ear a pure delight
    Not only in the sound, but in the sight!

ON NUMBERS

SONNETS FROM LAXENBURG: ON THE NUMBERS FROM ZERO TO TWELVE

ZERO

This is the greatest number of them all
Disguised as a mere point marking a graph
But underneath, a diabolic laugh,
An infinite abyss in which to fall
Of nothingness. No Thing can more appall
Than nothing—no, no rope, no rod, no staff
Can save us from what can't be done by half—
Where nothing is, there's no-one we can call.

But if there's anything, then there is hope,
For take the smallest thing, divide by zero,
And zoom! springs up infinity, the hero
That even with blank nothingness can cope
    For multiply infinity by nought
    And the vast finite universe is wrought.

ONE

Before the universes were begun
Beyond the furthest flights of mind and thought
In the great unimaginable, was there nought
Or was there, inconceivably, a One?
But back to earth—when all is said and done
How could arithmetic, or more, be taught
Except by one and one and one—so ought
Not one to be of all our thought the sun?

And here is mystery too—that I am many
Yet one in all my multitudinous parts
Like a great reel of patterned rope that darts
From birth to death. Yet neither I nor any
    One can conceive what power, or what Divinity
    Can make a One, out of a near-infinity.

TWO

Cleave the whole universe and make it Two
But careful! it can cleave at any place
And two is all we need, for sex, class, race
Talk, sneers, fights, love, to cherish or to rue.
With two, teachers can teach and lawyers sue.
Two can communicate from face to face,
Walk arm in arm, or part, or else embrace.
There seems no limit on what two can do!

Two can create new life, two can destroy.
A duel can turn two into one, or nought.
Two minus one is one, when prey is caught.
But one plus one makes three, when ones employ
    Ones one, and all alone, for ever more so
    But split it into two, and off we go!

e (2.71828)

Along the road, somewhere 'twixt two and three
There is a most strange monument to time
When roughly five-sevenths of the way you climb
You sense it, though its shape you cannot see.
Mathematicians call it simply "e".
It may seem to have no reason and less rhyme
But just put out to interest a thin dime
Continuously compounded, sleazily

Growing each moment at an annual rate
At which by simple interest it would double
In one year's time. Then, without any trouble
You'll find not two, but e dimes on your plate—
      Though nineteen-sevenths of a sum of money
      Only in mathematics isn't funny.

THREE

Two's company, and three, of course, a crowd.
Two can do much, but three can do much more.
Two love or fight—a third can keep the score.
Three make three different pairs, if that's allowed.
The odd one out may—or may not—be cowed,
But without three, where is the playwright's lore,
Who would we hiss, and who would we adore?
How could I know the sun, but for the cloud?

And then, of course, there is the trinity
Far beyond dialectics—First, Potential,
That must be realized in an essential
Script or score. That to be heard must be
    Played—with high spirit, if not always holy
    All in one pattern, yet Three, not one solely.

π (3.14159)

Nearly one-seventh of the way to four
We find another monument—a wheel
With a diameter we see and feel
And pace, and count how many steps we score
Then find the way all round is pi times more
Than the quick way across—but ah! how do we deal
With an unending number that is real?—
When we ourselves are finite to the core?

No wonder Indiana passed a law
To say pi should be three, to make things easy
For children in their schools—and for the queasy
Insist the Holy Bible has no flaw,
    For something in the Book of Kings is found
    Ten cubits straight across, and thirty round!

FOUR

Four winds, four seasons, phases of the moon,
Four legs to every table, every chair.
How solid it can seem to be foursquare!
And Four/Four common time makes a good tune.
Two shoot it out on Main Street at high noon
But to these scrappers add another pair
And we have tennis, where all's square and fair
And we have made a sportsman from a goon.

But careful now! Earth, Air, Water, and Fire
Were not enough. A fifth evangelist,
Found in a cave, might well improve the list.
The four grim horsemen bring disaster dire,
    And when the sharp command goes out "form fours,"
    Flee to the woods—it may be time for wars!

FIVE

Five for the symbols at your door:
Sight, hearing, taste, and touch, and smell.
Five arms the starfish has as well.
Our head, arms, legs add to no more.
In old rhymes, groups of three or four
The graces, fates, Blind Mice, all tell
Good tales, like the four horsemen fell,
But fives are nowhere in old lore.

But then there is the Pentagram
With five sharp points—a magic star
In which from Satan safe we are—
But even that is all a sham.
    Likewise we are defended not
    By Pentagon's five-sided plot.

SIX

Before we are at sevens, we are at sixes
A bit confused, past the simplicity
Of unity, or even two or three
Into the world of "many," where the mixes
Explode in number, past all simple fixes
And even statisticians can't agree
How to describe the complex shape we see
And randomness turns us all into pixies!

Still, thanks to old Chaldea, six still rules
Time's measurement in seconds, minutes, hours
Six tens, six twos, six fours display their powers
Over the clock, in all the different schools.
    Though inch and penny die on metric block
    Not even Frenchmen metricize the clock.

SEVEN

So now we come to seven, the lucky number
And groups in plenty to this banner flock.
Both deadly sins and cardinal virtues shock
The unexamined mind out of its slumber.
Salome's seven veils merely encumber
More elegantly than a strip-tease frock.
Seven dwarfs, lamps, wonders, all come out of stock
Like seven wives, sacks, cats, kits, and other lumber.

But there's more to it—seven, plus or minus
Is all that we can grasp in loose array
Or so, at least, psychologists all say
And six to eight seem best to wine and dine us
    And so the magic of the number seven
    May well have been produced in Plato's heaven.

EIGHT

After wild seven, eight is very square.
There's something prim about an octagon
The eightfold way for Buddhists still goes on
The square dance is what eight performers share.
When oddball numbers get into your hair
And make you feel a little put upon
Add one to them—they're even when you've done
And getting even with them's only fair.

But eight is more than square—it is a cube
Solidly sitting, two by two by two
While one by one by one is one—so do
We see how models all go down the tube
    For double lengths, and we increase the weight
    Of any structure, live or not, by eight.

NINE

The even numbers have a taste of earth
The odd take on a touch of things divine
And that perhaps is why there are muses nine
To guarantee that we will have no dearth
Of company, as with torment and mirth
We sketch and scribble, line by painful line
On our small canvas, the immense design
Of everything that has both truth and worth.

But nine, too, is a matrix, three by three,
Useful, indeed, for playing tic-tac-toe
But useful also when we want to show
All pairs involving A and B and C.
    And then we see—letting our minds take wing
    How everything reacts with everything.

TEN

Ah! now we see the double-digit bringers
And in the scale we use we're back again
To one and zero, when we come to ten
Only because we have ten toes or fingers
And mankind's early childhood habit lingers
Of holding up our outspread digits when
We want to show to those within the den
How many rabbits, foes, dancers, or singers.

Apart from that, the decimal is dismal:
It won't divide in quarters or in thirds
And, outside drinking, fifths are for the birds.
So counting tens is ignorance abysmal
    And we would do much better by ourselves
    If only we would learn to count in twelves!

ELEVEN

Eleven's a number that is hard to praise
It's only ten plus, or twelve minus one—
The first prime after seven—but where's the fun
In primeness—by itself it gets no "A's."
There is, indeed, the ancient ditty's phrase—
"Eleven that went to heaven"—but our minds run
Out to the twelfth, the unforgiven son
Of those never forgotten seven days.

Still, lost eleven has his glorious hour
For as the clock ticks on toward our doom,
Only the eleventh hour gives us any room
For hope, for time's arrest. Eleven's power
    Is what makes last the first, and sets all right,
    So midnight's curfew may not ring tonight!

TWELVE

Twelve is not only midnight, it is noon.
The sunlike ring of numbers round the face
Of time's instructor has the special grace
To halve, to quarter, like the measured moon.
It even grants us the unusual boon
Of parting into thirds. The human pace
Measures three human feet in any place
Twelve inches each; twelve months add to the tune.

Twelve intervals define all harmony
And even discord. What more could we ask
Of any number? So take up the task
Of Duodecimal Integrity
    And liberate the human race again
    From the mean metric of the number ten!

ON SCIENCE,
SCIENTISTS, AND TECHNOLOGY

SONNET FOR SCIENCE
16 March 1992

Even great scientists have made mistakes,
Which others—often pupils—have corrected;
Science at large expects the unexpected,
Unusual accidents and lucky breaks,
But what it cannot tolerate is fakes.
Lies and deceit, once they have been detected,
Are not forgiven. Totally ejected
From the professions are the found-out rakes.

Another principle that must pervade
The realm of science is that change in views
Must never come from those who threats will use;
Only the power of evidence must persuade.
    And freedom to explore and to debate
    Must be enjoyed, or science will stagnate.

SONNET FOR THE
CATHEDRAL OF SCIENCE
5 April 1992

Science is a cathedral of our minds,
It rises up, and out, to galaxies,
With space-time roofed before infinities,
But yet a vast, vast universe it finds.
And then it turns within, to seek what binds
Atoms, electrons, quarks, with subtle keys
In matter's miracle, while energies
And structures trade in many different kinds.

Beyond all this is life, and information,
Which patterns growth, from seed into the flower,
From egg to body and brain—amazing power!
As Founding Fathers can produce a nation!
    We know that a cathedral is not God,
    But is a footprint where Creation trod.

SONNET FOR THE
WOMB OF SCIENCE
6-7 March 1992

Copernicus was a cathedral canon.
Galileo was a good Catholic
All of his life, despite the dirty trick
The popes played on him: accusations ran on
Until the Church with cruelty put a ban on
The publishing of visions scientific.
Lutheran Kepler never ceased to stick
To church. Earth moved, but had both God and Man on.

Boyle, a devout Episcopalian,
Spent life and fortune to defend his views.
And why did Newton, done with physics, choose
To write tomes on the thoughts of Arian?
 It's clear that modern science had its birth
 In the womb of the Christian part of earth.

EVOLUTION

9 February 1985

The Universe is not much like a clock;
The circling planets fool us; they keep time
Only in this our brief, brief human clime,
At anchor in the solar system's dock.
When life appears it lets loose a great flock
Of wild improbabilities; not rhyme
Nor reason then are worth a dime;
What counts is not stability, but shock!

The time when most improbable events
Like DNA or *Homo sapiens*
Happen, in one of trillion trillion whens
Is why we are here now. What large intents
    Govern us, we know not. But this we see,
    A universe, magnificently free.

SONNET FOR COPERNICUS
25 February 1992

It's obvious to watchers of the sky
That every day the stars go round the earth,
In a great sphere of fairly modest girth,
And that the sun, the moon, and planets fly
Among the stars in circles that too lie
Around our solid world, and there's no dearth
Of measurements that justify the worth
Of this view of the heaven's majesty.

Then comes Copernicus, a humble canon,
Who says "What's obvious may not be true"
(An ancient Greek, perhaps, took a like view)
"The earth rotates and circles." Popes put a ban on
    This heresy. But Telescopic scan
    Soon made the obvious, Copernican.

SONNET FOR
TYCHO BRAHE AND KEPLER
29 February 1992

Tycho Brahe, a rather bumptious Dane,
Talked his king into giving him a place
Where every cloudless night he gazed at space,
Measuring each planet's place, again, again.
Then when the noble king had ceased to reign,
He went to Prague, and helped great Kepler trace
The elliptic paths where earth and planets race
Around the sun, pulled by its mighty chain.

Tycho still yearned to put beloved earth
At the great system's center, but the force
Of Kepler's model spelled the future course
Of every planet perfectly. The worth
    Of good Copernicus's dangerous view,
    Then became undisputable, as true.

SONNET FOR ISAAC NEWTON
2 March 1992

How strange it is when all things fall together,
And partial visions turn into a whole,
Magnetic ideas turn toward a pole,
Yet no one knows quite how, or why, or whether.
But so it was with Newton—a bellwether,
Leading diverse ideas toward a goal,
The apple from the tree, the planet's roll,
All bound by gravity, a single tether.

And yet behind the equations, the clear proof,
The all-encompassing power of constant "G,"
There still remained a kernel of mystery,
Something unsolved, invisible, aloof.
    So, even in Newton's life we come to see
    That after Science comes Theology.

IN AN AIRPORT
26 January 1992

Waiting, in a great airport, for my flight,
Looking out on the runways I see planes,
One by one, taking off along the lanes,
Into the blue sky and the sunset light.
However often seen, it's still a sight
That is amazing: wonder never wanes
As, from slow starts in speed and power, each gains
And shoots into the sky with sheer delight.

Around the runway flies a graceful bird;
But planes are made—and flown—by brains, not genes.
The mighty blast of power that gives them means
For flight is fed from ancient earth, deferred
    From earlier sun, turned into finite fuel.
    In time, planes stilled will be, and birds will rule.

San Francisco Airport

ON NATURE

SONNET FOR THE TURNING EARTH
21 January 1993

How good it is to live on Earth that turns,
That endlessly repeats the simple play
That gives us the great plot of night and day,
Sunrise, noontide, and sunset, and so earns
For us the precious skill that learns
To see the patterns in time's brave display
And so prevents our plans from going astray,
So we don't dash into a fire that burns.

Good it is too that Earth goes round the sun
In annual cycles, giving blessed seasons
So that we search successfully for reasons
Even though in some patterns we may see none.
    So it is clear that what makes human worth
    At least in part is learned from Mother Earth.

EARLIEST DAWN
22 November 1992, 6:15 a.m.

The storm is over and the air is clear
The mountains stand out in the earliest dawn
Patterned with snow and trees like a great scarf drawn
Over broad shoulders. Snowy roofs appear
Lighter than sky, lit with the snow's pale smear;
Below them, a faint square of lawn whitened.
No doubt at all a new day's being born
A line of latitude pops up— right here!

Being a modern man I know, of course,
It is the earth that rotates, not the sun,
The east horizon sinks, sun's rise is done.
The west horizon gobbles up the sky.
   Or is it only brain's chronic romance
   That sees the morn with astronomic glance?

SONNET FOR A TOWN ASLEEP
(AUGSBURG, BAVARIA)
22 March 1992

There is a magic in a town asleep.
Among a thousand windows only one
Shines, with an eerie light. Has day begun,
Or is there a crying child, or anguish deep?
On the dark street two empty buses creep;
Across the road a woman starts to run.
Silence enshrouds; no laughter and no fun
Are heard. Yet have I no desire to weep,

For eastward, round the earth, rushes the dawn,
And soon the light will come, the town will wake,
Laughter will pierce the silence, bodies shake
And move in their great game, both king and pawn.
    Earth never sleeps, for only half's in night,
    And who would want an endless year of light!

SONNET FOR AN ANT
15 July 1991

As I was stretched out, meditating, in my tub
An ant was crawling up the blue tiled wall;
For us, the Matterhorn would be as tall,
For those whose hobby is a climbing club.
Yet the brave ant climbed on without a flub,
How could a creature climb so high, so small?
It reached the ceiling; started then to crawl
Along the boundary. I could only dub

The creature crazy. It climbed down again
And up another wall. About half way,
Its body saying, "That's enough today,"
It stopped, exhausted—so far from its den.
    Humans—the thought is slightly melancholy—
    Are not the only form of life with folly!

SONNET FOR A BLIZZARD
10 March 1992

Under two feet of freshly fallen snow
We realize how vulnerable we are;
The lights go dark; clocks stop; our servant car
No longer can be used; we cannot go
To any usual place. The night skies glow
Faintly through mist. The near has become far,
Familiar earth is like a distant star,
And what was fast is now creepingly slow.

Yet what contracts in space expands in time;
I sense what lives were like before my own;
I can commune with times I have not known,
And sense the feeling of an earlier clime.
    So thank you, snow, for all that I have felt,
    And that you, too, are surely going to melt!

(With apologies to Whittier's "Snowbound.")

SNOW IN APRIL

9 April 1989

The flocking birds dot the great snowy tree,
The bending branches throw snow to the ground
In dancing showers. There is so little sound
I almost hear the winging that I see.
But it is Spring! Leaves striving to be free
Break into bud. Though beauty's all around
It is of sleep. Sleep cannot be profound
In time of rising sap—Winter must flee!

And so it will. The warm earth melts the snow
And turns it into nourishment of life.
So love will melt the icy grip of strife,
And peace will flower in the sun's blessed glow.
    One small degree above the freezing point,
    And snow will melt, and water will anoint.

SONNET FOR EARLY SPRING
20 April 1992

No time's as beautiful as early spring,
When half the trees are showing a light green,
But the leaves don't obscure the distant scene,
And dark trunks still are patterning.
Previous rains and early snow-melts bring
Turbulent rivers—not, of course, too clean,
But oh! what energy! Some small birds preen
Themselves busily before taking wing.

Above all else, the landscape is alive,
And over it there seems to be a glow
Of precious expectation, and we know
That circling earth will not take long to drive
    Winter away, giving us good reasons
    To glory in the drama of the seasons.

SONNET FOR THE LONGEST DAY

21 June 1991

The summer solstice has a sadness in it,
Even if it's a perfect summer's day.
The year, relentlessly upon its way,
Has reached a turning point. Minute by minute,
Each coming day will have less sun within it,
Until in bleak December, cold and gray,
The repetitious melody will play,
Interminable, if not infinite.

And so in life. The brightest happiness
Presages subtly sorrows yet to come:
But there's another side; sorrow's grim drum
Is prelude to a greater joy, not less,
     And time is something we can come to see
     As but the shadow of infinity.

In my office in Boulder.

TO LONG'S PEAK

8 February 1986

Your Majesty! I look at you in awe.
I have to raise my eyes and crick my neck
To see your head. My body's but a speck
Before your massive cliffs. A jagged saw
Of skyline cuts the sky, and a white claw
Of snowfield rakes the rocks. The distant deck
That makes your top is shadowed by the fleck
Of crowning clouds. You know nothing of flaw.

But I have stood on your top's rocky brink
With arms upstretched in triumph of a kind.
Your majesty is wholly in my mind,
Your rule is only to erode and shrink.
　　But so rule human kings. Your majesty
　　Is no less real for being found in me.

Aspen Lodge, Estes Park, Colorado, at the Rocky Mountain Program of the University of Colorado at Denver's Center for the Improvement of Public Management.

SONNET FOR BOULDER CREEK
17-18 May 1992

The waters in the creek go "Hurry, Hurry!"
As if they cannot wait to reach the sea,
The place they pass is lovely as can be,
And yet they seem to be in such a worry!
The waves stay put—only the waters scurry,
As if to some great destiny they flee.
Their boss, of course, is constant Gravity,
Whose favor, surely, there's no need to curry.

But then, what right have I the creek to scold
When my own life has been a constant motion
Toward what?—not even an ocean
But just toward the time of getting old.
    Still, I have much enjoyed what I have done,
    So maybe you, stream, are just having fun!

SONNET FOR LAKE HURON
3 July 1992

Great Lakes indeed are cousins of the sea
But have a quality that's all their own.
They whisper to us with a modest tone,
Long waves roll into shore quite silently
With something of a gentle dignity.
Storms and high winds are by no means unknown,
But not too long after the winds have blown
The waves return to their tranquility.

The water's fresh; that may contribute to
The sense of humanness, for salty stuff,
Though good for some things, does taste rather rough,
And freshness is a virtue to pursue.
    So I am grateful for this earthly treasure
    That can inspire such pure and gentle pleasure.

ON HUMAN NATURE

SONNET FOR EDEN
26 May1992

Somewhere, there was an Adam and an Eve,
Or else the human race would not be here.
Somewhere in time and space, Edens appear,
Deep memories linger, making us believe.
Then, too, Edens are lost. Though we may grieve,
The trees of knowledge grow. Both joy and fear
Enter the world, bringing both laugh and tear,
Humans gain power to learn, and to achieve.

So, every simple heaven on earth will perish,
Knowledge will grow and, with knowledge, power
For good or ill. Disastrous storms will lower,
Threatening the goodness that we cherish.
    Yet storms pass, and for us it is essential
    To hold that good's the ultimate potential.

SONNET FOR EXTRAORDINARY LIVES
19 November 1992

Beyond the daily lives that we all share,
The days, weeks, months, and seasons that sail by,
There are events that hit us in the eye
That are both strangely powerful and rare.
We common people may deem things unfair
That give so few such power, but can't deny
Great names that dot the page of history,
And cannot possibly be torn from there.

The test is simple: Had they died at birth
Jesus and Galileo, Newton, those
Because of whose lives human knowledge grows,
We now would see a very different earth.
    Because of them our ordinary lives
    Grow richer, and human potential thrives.

SONNET FOR THE MODERN WORLD
11 March 1992

I must confess myself a citizen
Of the blatant world of modernity.
Some of its aspects—its complexity,
Its dominance—make me feel alien,
Longing, perhaps, for simpler worlds again,
Disturbed by world-wide uniformity,
Destroying local life in its variety,
Drowning all ancient lands in a vast new sea.

And yet I can't renounce my citizenship,
For I am part of that enormous growth
In knowledge, based on evidence, not oath,
That made the world that has us in its grip.
    Ignorance cannot save us—we must find
    Knowledge in all the lives of humankind.

SONNET FOR FUTURES

23 February 1992

If I am asked where the world's future lies,
I have to answer that I do not know,
For there are many ways where it might go,
And none are certain, all will bring surprise,
And some we will deplore, and some will prize.
Yet the long course of time's mysterious flow
Human decisions can affect, and show
Some patterns that the use of power implies.

But what is power, and what is impotence,
What is illusory, what realistic,
What is too narrow, what too synergistic,
What images are nonsense, what make sense?
    These questions we must never cease to ask,
    If better futures are to be our task.

SONNET FOR GENES
26 March 1992

I have no doubt that my whole life began
In a small fertile egg within a womb
That had Potential—not for a single doom
But for more lives than any mind could scan.
It certainly had something like a plan
To weave my life on its enormous loom,
But it would be presumptuous to assume
That from this warp only one pattern ran.

Of all the countless lives I could have lived,
Only one turned into reality,
Guided by chance, by others, and by me,
And through my images of futures sieved.
    So, in this world of chance, pushes, and pulls,
    All lives, including mine, are miracles.

SONNET FOR
GENES, RACE, AND GENDER
15 May 1992

Our genes make us a single human race.
We share what makes our bones, our blood, our brain,
Our body organs. Differences remain
In shade of skin, some features of the face
But these come from a very minor place,
A minute fraction of the mighty train
Of DNA that builds us, grain by grain,
Whose pattern one day we may hope to trace.

Genes are important—some genetic quirk
Makes half the babies female, the rest male,
But then, the rest of the genetic tale
In terms of whole potential—this we shirk.
    A gene can be a blesser or offender;
    These spread at random, not by race or gender.

SONNET FOR GENETICS
2 June 1992

In view of all the countless genes we share
All men, quite literally, are my brother,
All women, like my sisters or my mother,
Going right back to the ancestral pair.
The genes that foster love and tender care
And pushed our forebears into being lovers,
We share with them. Then there are many others
That everyone's uniqueness have to bear.

The genes that give us gender, color, race
Are but a tiny fraction of the whole;
In many ways we share a single soul.
These basic facts our cultures have to face:
    If we deny humanity to any,
    We do it to ourselves, for each is many.

ON WAR, PEACE, ANGER, HATE

SONNET FOR
FIGHTING AND CURING
15 June 1992

Why are we so obsessed with fighting ills,
When what we really need to do is cure!
Fighting's dramatic, and has great allure,
But isn't very good at changing wills.
Curing is much more complex. It instills
Changes within the body that endure.
We can't, indeed, ever be wholly sure,
And every sickness can't be cured by pills!

If we assume that someone is to blame
For every ill, and all we have to do
Is name, and kill them off—then evils new
Will rise from where the older evils came.
   Only by finding truth about the past,
   Will curing be discovered that will last.

SONNET FOR SECURITY

2 February 1992

Why should a passion for security
Drive us toward increasing armament,
Divorcing the real future from intent,
Creating hopes with little surety?
How can we grow toward maturity,
Where humankind no longer will be rent
By useless conflict, but will find assent
In common truth, real in its purity?

Security's the father of stagnation—
It is the insecure who innovate,
They must live dangerously who would create!
Security produces no elation
    To be both fully human and secure
    We must know how to love, and how to cure.

College House, Christchurch, New Zealand

SONNET FOR POLAND

September 1988

I am in Warsaw, Nineteen Eighty-Eight.
I wander through the streets, but half alive
To the events of Forty-Four or -Five,
And find a little church, of modern date.
There, on a wall, each on a slab of slate
Are names, names, names, that shockingly revive
The memory of how we humans could connive
At death, destruction, despicable hate.

I enter. Mass is starting. Simple folk
With lined, sad faces worship. A young priest
Performs the spotless rite. The war has ceased.
The land is searching for an easier yoke.
    I am immeasurably moved. I weep
    For joy and sorrow, lost—and rescued—sheep.

SONNET FOR
CHOICE AMONG EVILS
29 April 1992

The greatest moral agony is choice
Between two evils—going toward either
Pushes us to the other, so that neither
Can beckon us with a commanding voice,
Leaving us, where we never can rejoice,
In hopeless doubt, continuing to cry there,
Without the crippled spirit getting lither,
Getting no message, hearing only noise.

Should we expel a fetus that, if born,
Would live a life of misery and pain?
Should we prolong life when that life is vain?
Should we, when fighting wars, all mercy scorn,
    Denying to the foe humanity,
      In the pursuit of empty victory?

FOR QUEEN VICTORIA

4 March 1990

A plumber's son, a blacksmith's grandson, I
Find myself in the palace of a Queen,
A Princess Royal, an Empress. All unseen,
Ghosts of a past age silently slip by.
Within my imagination's world I try
To be with, to become them, and to glean
Some little sense of what they must have been
In that so near, so distant, bye and bye.

Did she, Victoria, love her Emperor son,
Whose pride brought Europe down in blood and flame,
And did her widowed mind feel pride—or shame—
Did she feel but a pawn whose game was done?
    How strange that walls, built in another age,
    Should with such poignancy my mind engage!

Schlosshotel Kronberg, Frankfurt, Germany

SONNET FOR PEACE
22 January 1992

All peace that is imposed on earth by war
Is nothing but submission. It is frail.
Threat creates counterthreat, an endless trail
Of meaningless destruction, hate and gore,
Breeding upon itself, more and still more.
As fertile minds find new means to assail
All old defenses, all defense will fail
And over all the earth red death will pour.

Peace is a habit of the human mind;
It can be cultivated, practised, taught,
'Til useless violence shrinks itself to nought,
And war is something we have left behind.
    Conflict, indeed, will not and should not cease,
    But will creative be when wrapped in peace.

EARLY DAWN
20 November 1992

How long it takes the sky to become light
On a November morn! The pace of change
Is not perceptible within the range
Of five long, waiting minutes—yet no fright
Assaults the heart—in ten minutes the bright
Is clearly on the way. Nothing is strange.
At steady pace the light and dark exchange
And day, slow but peaceful, conquers the night.

And so it is with human peace and war.
Peace is a day that dawns, however slow,
Until the thought of war receives a "No"
With the slow growth of habit and of law.
    Analogies should be pursued with care
    But still, truth always has some footprints there.

FOR DAWN
4 April 1990

How dark, how dark it is before the dawn!
The deathlike silence of eternity
Blankets the void. I nothing hear, or see.
Only soft touch tells me that I was born.
Of life and hope I feel untimely shorn.
And then! Through the deep dark, quite suddenly,
A bird begins to sing. Vacancies flee,
Presaging joy, the first glad glimpse of morn.

So in the darkness of the long, long night
Of poverty, and misery, and war,
Our burdened minds and hearts break out, and soar
To sound of song, telling of dawn's delight,
    For those who sing of oneness and of peace
    Tell us that dawn will come, and darkness cease.

Schlosshotel Kronberg, Frankfurt, Germany

SONNET FOR THE
LEARNING OF PEACE

27 February 1992

In every discipline of human learning
We can't teach students what we do not know
And if the things we think we know aren't so,
We won't deserve the income we are earning.
And so, to more research we should be turning,
Not just to find truth, but keep error low,
And make the light of curiousness grow,
And keep the spirit of inquiry burning.

Now, when the world so desperately needs peace,
We all need endlessly to learn and teach,
And teach and learn, as far as we can reach,
To make cruel war decline, and peace increase.
    For peace, with all the blessings in its train,
    Comes from unused potential in our brain.

Written at the Peace Studies Association 4th Annual Conference, University of Colorado at Boulder

SONNET FOR HEALING

15 March 1992

A finger cut is healed within a week,
A broken bone is healed within a year,
A cutting word takes longer—we prefer
To keep the mind's wounds open—a mystique
Of battle makes the healing hard to seek
And memories of old wounds, like a burr,
Constantly prick. We drink the bitter myrrh
Of endless war, making all futures bleak.

But when the body's healing fails, we turn
To hospitals, physicians, medicines,
Pharmacists, surgeons—not to cure our sins,
But heal our bodies. Surely we can learn
    To build healing professions, skilled in curing
    The social ills we've been too long enduring.

SONNET FOR THE HUMAN BRAIN
19 March 1992, 4 a.m.

A human brain can have as many cells
As there are stars within our galaxy
And what is even more, it can be free
To ring the changes on its billion bells.
We can't take in what mathematics tells—
The numbers rise toward infinity
That measure the potentiality
Of this enormous universe that wells

Up from the brain, and turns it into mind.
But why, oh why, does this great universe
So often turn from better toward the worse?
We look for good, and then so often find
    Error, deceit, hate, cruelties. Do we trace
    Too much potential here, too little grace?

SONNET FOR THE
RIOTS IN LOS ANGELES, 2 MAY 1992
2 May 1992

There are too many things we take for granted—
That those who do the wrong will bear the blame,
And after that, things will be much the same,
Mistaken views will somehow be recanted,
The protest songs will peacefully be chanted,
Even the poor will go on playing the game
That keeps them powerless, with acceptance tame,
And seeds of peace will somehow be replanted.

And then, quite suddenly, there comes a cliff
Over which angry, screaming faces fall,
And the once peaceful, busy shopping mall
Becomes a looting, flaming hell, as if
    A lid were lifted off a hidden fire,
    Fueled by an old, suppressed, and re-lit ire.

IN GALILEE

23 January 1989

Always there is something, something beyond;
Beyond defeat and victory, beyond strife,
Beyond the past, the present, beyond life,
Beyond the armor that we all have donned,
Beyond the best that all our minds have conned,
Beyond the bomb, the gun, the stone, the knife,
Beyond the altar, flag, the drum and fife,
Beyond the awful slough of foul despond,

Beyond all night there is the glim of dawn,
Beyond even the end of all our rope
There spring the great improbable wings of hope,
Beyond the dying, stinking fish—there's spawn.
    Beyond the pain, the fear, the claw, the tooth
    There is forgiveness, healing, love, and truth.

Written while attending the Conference on War, Peace, and Geography, University of Haifa, Israel.

IN THE WASHINGTON
NATIONAL ARBORETUM
20 September 1985

Here, in the midst of the metropolis
Whose muscled statues boast of cruel might,
There is a place of quiet, where the light
Filters through treetops with the gentlest kiss.
The dry leaves rustle with a half-heard hiss
When beech nuts drop upon them from the height;
Distant birds sing with uncontrolled delight;
My restless mind calms to a still, cool bliss.

And in the storm of anger and of hate
That drives this city toward its final doom,
O God! Let there be found one secret room
Where arrogant power can catch the voice of fate,
  Whispering through the clamor, "I have news!
  There is another road. You still can choose."

ON SOCIAL SCIENCE

SONNET FOR ALCHEMY
18 March 1992

What we inherited from alchemy—
The laboratory, the experiment,
The unremitting search for what is meant
By matter's structure—this is history
That should not be despised. Yet now we see
They had no real successes. Their intent
To make gold failed. What they called element,
Earth, water, air, and fire, we now agree

Are mixtures, processes, through which may pass
True elements. Water is H_2O,
Earth is an ecosystem, fire a glow
From some reaction, air a flow of gas.
    But social science is still alchemy—
    The gold of peace and justice we don't see.

SONNET FOR SIGMUND FREUD
1 April 1992

Sigmund Freud dreamed he saw unconscious mind,
And, like Columbus, set off across a dark
Tempestuous emptiness, on a frail barque
Of Consciousness, to see what he could find.
He found something: islands, perhaps, that lined
An unknown continent where Noah's Ark
Had never rested. What he found was stark
And made him, to the land behind it, blind.

The territories of all human brains,
Peaks, troughs, great forests, fertile fields,
Which vast variety of harvests yields:
Science, Religion, Beauty, Love, and Pain.
    He did not venture there, but chose to explore
    A little island lying off the shore.

SONNET FOR JUSTICE
28 March 1992

But what is Justice? How I wish I knew!
My heart yearns for it, but my brain demurs;
What should be tolerated, what incurs
Reproach? What things are straight, and what askew?
What visions are imperfect, what are true?
Equality is a great hope that stirs—
Especially when what's his should be hers—
But doubts cling to the searching mind like burrs.

Lottery tickets are a clear demand
For Inequality—but gambling's vice.
In sport we think being the "best" is nice,
And a conductor has to lead a band.
    Yet here's a theorem no one can refute—
    The heart of Justice is its own pursuit.

In Cincinnati Airport

SONNET FOR THE NEIGHBORHOOD
DEMOCRATIC CAUCUS
14 April 1992

They come—a somewhat miscellaneous group
Of people gathered from the neighborhood.
Some may be naive—some are fairly good
At jumping through the somewhat twisted hoop
Of politics—not getting in the soup
Of disagreement, finding where they stood
On touchy issues that might mean they could
Lose the election; learning when to stoop,

And when to stand against a blatant wrong,
When to be quiet, when a little raucous,
And how to turn a heterogeneous caucus
Into a choir, singing the same good song.
    So, to democracy all should be turning
    When it is not just voting, but group learning.

ON HIS CAREER

SONNET FOR ECONOMICS

24 June 1992

Economist for all my working days,
I should by this time roughly know what's best
For humankind, and put to some small test
My colleagues' images of yeas and nays.
The economy, however, is a maze;
To map it is a very complex quest.
Even its history mostly must be guessed
So, over this great ignorance we raise

A fantasy of markets with perfection,
Mistaking charm and elegance for truth:
But Error has a penetrating tooth
That bites when we go in a false direction.
    And if our theories are mainly fictions,
    It's most unwise to make exact predictions!

ON READING
A BIOGRAPHICAL DICTIONARY
OF DISSENTING ECONOMISTS
24 March 1992

Reading about the lives and works of thinkers,
Even within the walls of my own field,
I must to a rather sad conviction yield,
That there is much I don't see through my blinkers.
And even though some thoughts out there are stinkers,
The knowledge that within my mind is sealed
Is such a tiny part of what's revealed
In all five billion minds. But my mind tinkers

With the idea that only what is true
Is good. Yet error skillfully embeds
Itself so quickly in so many heads
That there is much I'm glad I never knew,
    And I can add, perhaps, a little whine,
      That so few other heads know what's in mine!

SONNET FOR THE NOÖSPHERE

28 March 1992

I

All my life I have been teacher and taught,
Working to transfer into other minds
Ideas and images that searching finds
In the wide landscape of my inner thought.
And this to me has much contentment brought.
I could have lived long lives of other kinds,
And yet, somehow, the stream of life that winds
Through space and time has not borne me for naught.

The final purpose of the universe
Is not for us to know: but here and now
We know that we can nourish and endow,
From the rich content of our own mind's purse,
    The knowledge universe that grows and spreads
    Through past, present, and future human heads.

Miami University, Oxford, Ohio

SONNET FOR THE NOÖSPHERE
13 March 1992

II

Our precious earth is made of many spheres,
Rocks, water, air, life, and the human race;
Each interacts with each, each has a place,
Endlessly changing with the passing years.
But now, something remarkable appears:
A sphere of knowledge, images that trace
Through human minds the patternings that lace
The real world; small?—large! and distant?—near!

But knowledge, like all things, passes away,
As we forget, and as we ourselves die,
And must be born, in young minds, constantly,
By teaching, learning, thinking, testing, play.
    And to extinction will frail knowledge go,
      Unless they who know, teach, and who teach, know.

SONNET FOR AN OASIS
3 January 1992

Long in the country of the active mind
I have been traveling with tireless feet,
Seeking my fellow travelers to greet
With tales of all the wonders there to find.
And though in devious ways the paths may wind,
Still there are many grateful pastures sweet
And moments when the journey seems complete
When all converge on points that Truth assigned.

And sometimes there are lonely deserts where
I shouted into emptiness, until
Some caravan appeared over the hill
And saved me from aloneness and despair.
    And so I find my intellectual place is
    Not the whole universe, but an oasis.

American Economic Association, New Orleans

SONNET FOR SELF-PITY
16 January 1992

I have built up great castles in the sand,
That wind and waves have swiftly leveled low,
And in the bustling crowd I loudly blow
The trumpet of my thoughts, without a hand
To clap, or ear to hear in all the land.
My words and writings like a river flow
That disappears into the sand below,
A great supply for which there's no demand.

Ah well! Perhaps I am before my time,
And after I am safely gone from earth
Some prying scholar will expose the worth
Of truths that were not noticed in my prime.
    But yet, whate'er the future thinks I've done,
    Blowing my trumpet has been lots of fun!

SONNET FOR PRAISE

17 January 1992

Costs we know fairly well, but benefits
Are vague, obscure. Money, we must confess,
Has a nice quality of more or less,
Even when in a distant bank it sits.
But the net worth of praise takes all our wits
To calculate; and it is hard to guess
What people mean by honors, when they dress
Them up in gowns, hoods, calligraphic writs.

Perhaps the best reward is just a smile
A flash of understanding in the eye,
The recognition of a passer-by,
The handshake in a warm and friendly style.
 Yet all these fade before the satisfaction
 Of turning one's potential into action.

SONNET FOR BEING APOLITICAL
25 March 1992

Has my life been too apolitical?
I never walked the corridors of power,
And when the world's great storm clouds start to lower,
Do I hide in the analytical?
Of governments I have been critical,
Before the nation-state I do not cower,
Though I do pay my taxes! But the flower
Of human life is not the citadel.

I seek the power of truth, not that of threat,
Propped up by anthems and by sacrifice;
So do I just stand by, giving advice,
Which no one seems to listen to as yet?
    I knock on the closed door of polity,
    But conscience nags—should I have turned the key?

TO MY DESKTOP
5-6 May 1992

My desktop is an appalling clutter
Of things unread, unanswered, every one
Reminding me of things I haven't done,
Of thought unthought and words I didn't utter.
And all I ever seem to do is putter.
I deal with some things, then what seems a ton
Of mail comes in—I'm tempted then to run,
My mind feels like an overflowing gutter.

I can't decide whether I need more time
Or do I need a more determined will?
But change in will's an order hard to fill,
And nothing stops the clock's relentless chime.
    But whether I can find the will—oh, well!
    That is a story only time can tell.

ON FAITH

SONNET FOR CREATION
20 February 1992

I know there is creation. I created,
By my own self, over an active life,
With fingers, mind, pen, paper, saw, and knife,
Objects, books, sonnets, thoughts that can be dated.
Some quite original; some imitated.
And I, together with my precious wife,
With love—and just a little touch of strife—
Created five new humans, all now mated,

And in their turn creating. Through all time
Creation prospers. What, then, of the start?
Is a Creator at creation's heart,
A Rhymer without which there is no rhyme?
    But only Faith, and Faith's imagination
    Can sense the Great Creator of creation.

SONNET FOR THANKS

28 December 1991

How can I thank the Creator of all Creation,
For the uncountable blessing of my life,
In work, in friends, in offspring, and in wife?
Thanks are expressions of a power relation,
A sign of inequality in station,
Ways for the weaker to encounter strife
More powerfully than with the gun or knife,
With conflict covered up by integration.

But holy love—that's quite another matter;
It is an ocean that embraces all,
Without a trace of weakness or of gall,
Binding in liquid grace all that could scatter.
    In holy love alone can we give thanks
    Free from all stain of status or of ranks.

SONNET FOR THE WALLS OF TIME
26 September 1983

I

All we have is traces, tracks, and no mind
Knows what hooves, what wheels, what wing-tips made
These scratches on time's sands: but all obeyed
One Law, that everywhere we chance to find
Clear traces in succession, well defined.
Something has passed that way, something has laid
Marks on blank earth, and something has betrayed
Its presence by the past it left behind.

So in our minds are traces. Galloping fears
Leave deep, deep scars. Time's chariot's ruthless tracks
Deepen with age, until our whole world cracks.
But also in the dust the trace appears
    Of wing-tips; ah! it is the blessed dove,
    Visiting us with faith, and hope, and love.

SONNET FOR THE WALLS OF TIME
26 September 1983

II

Is God then dead? Do echoes die away?
Shaman and priest and prophet, Lord and Christ
That in their time with bell and rod enticed
The human sheep to countenance their sway,
And at their bid to worship and to pray:
Are they then from their ancient triumphs sliced,
Frozen with chilly reason, safely iced
In the great glacier of the modern day?

Or could it be indeed that *we* are dead,
Embalmed in empty reason's subtle chill?
Or are we just in deep-freeze? One day, will
New fires of love from heart to icy head
    Produce a resurrection, and a thaw,
    And flower in deeper wonder, holier awe?

SONNET FOR THE WALLS OF TIME
26 September 1983

III

If all the world's a stage, what then's the play,
And what our little part? At first we bawl,
Then smile, suck, stretch, turn over, stand and crawl,
Toddle and stride, then strut, jog, run, till day
Dawns when we totter, then in death still stay.
Meanwhile the play goes on, including all
The crumpled stage of this blue shining ball,
Four billion actors in a random fray.

But somewhere in the caverns of the mind
There is a prompter's box. Can we forget,
For one still moment, tumult, shouting, fret,
And listen? Then our inward ear may find
    Not the great plot—that is beyond our art—
    But subtle intimations of our part.

SONNET FOR THE WALLS OF TIME
26 September 1983

IV

The skin breaks on our bursting chrysalis,
And out comes—not a soaring butterfly
To carry us to some diviner sky,
But just another chrysalis. We miss
The great fulfillment and the final bliss,
But keep on eating, growing, and rely
On crawling on green leaves to get us by,
Without even the promise of a kiss.

And if the End is nothing, Way is all,
We may accept the wisdom of the Tao;
But there's a growing frown upon the brow
When all the Way permits is but a crawl.
 And who can blame us if some sweet voice sings,
 Within the sober chrysalis, of wings!

Written on planes between Denver and Syracuse, New York, while reading
John E. Whiteford Boyle, "Graffiti on the Wall of Time."

SONNET FOR LIGHT

9 March 1986

Often at night, stumbling into my room
My hand fumbles the wall toward the switch
And in a flash I am become light-rich;
Miraculously vanished is the gloom.
But then, I see! Across my desk a flume
Of tumbled papers floods—and most of which
I should be reading, answering; but I itch
Not for the duties that I should assume.

So, when the light within my twilit soul
Flares suddenly, in worship, or in prayer,
I fear to see what is illumined there
For it is hard to rise from Part to Whole,
    And I am weak. But answer I must try;
    There is no eyelid for the inward eye.

In 15th Street Friends Meeting, New York City

GERMANTOWN MEETING
June 1984

Since earth was formed, the stars and galaxies
Have spoken to it, silently, in waves
Of light, in structured radiance that laves
In language, blind, deaf continents and seas;
'Til consciousness, emerging by degrees,
Breaks into knowing human mind that craves
To translate every message that engraves
Itself sense, 'til mind with truth agrees.

And why? We have a universe within
With cells as numerous as are the stars
But closer, in communion. They can parse
The grammar of the sky, and knowledge win.
    The inward light how great! The still, small voice
    How clear! What does it say? Rejoice, Rejoice!

TRANSPARENCY
19 May 1987

How precious always is transparency!
Our senses are dark windows through which come
Into mind's empty rooms rumors of some
Vast worlds outside that are reality.
Touch we trust best. But what we hear and see
Stirs up our thoughts, keeps us from being numb,
Creates whole inner worlds, makes our minds hum
And flash with learning and activity.

But let us not despise opaqueness either;
The perfectly transparent can't be seen.
All would dissolve in light were there no screen,
No shade, no wall, no skin, no silence. Neither
    Pure blinding light can teach us, nor black dark.
    Trumpets make deaf. To a still, small voice, we hark.

Sydney, New South Wales, Australia

TREES IN THE WIND
30 March 1985, 8:30 a.m.

Trees in the wind—how gratefully they bow,
An exquisitely honest form of prayer,
Submission laced with thanks but unaware
As far as our stiff minds and thoughts allow.
The bowing's but mechanics. We endow
The wind with will, as if it chose to care
Whither and when and what it blows, and where,
And by command making the trees kow-tow.

And in the endless forest of the mind
We think we choose, and bow, and praise, and pray,
Direct our course toward another day,
And seek, and seek, and seek, and sometimes find.
    Magnetic gales blow through our tangled cells;
    But we are there—only if God there dwells.

At 115 Oakmont Place, San Antonio, Texas

SONNET FOR A MISTY MORNING

27 May 1992

Clothed in a thick mist, uniformly gray,
Familiar mountains disappear from sight,
Yet, in imagination's inward light
I tell my eyes exactly where they lay,
And I am sure that later, perhaps today,
The mist will pass, the sun will then be bright,
And show the mountains have not taken flight,
For they, in our time, cannot pass away.

So, passing through the darkness of the soul,
When Divine Love is hidden in the mist,
We know, beyond the cloud, it does exist,
And that the shroud of mist away will roll,
 For clouds can hide, but never can destroy,
 The everlasting sun of blessed joy.

FROM PENDLE HILL
14 November 1988

Do acorns imagine the great oak trees
That in their cells they know how to create?
Can fertile eggs imagine the life's fate
Of what comes from them by such slow degrees?
Pots are in potters' minds before they seize
The amorphous clay, and poems elevate
The poet's thoughts before they pass the gate
Of skin, and on cold pen and paper freeze.

Imagination's bounds we never reach,
Not even at the farthest galaxy;
A universe of glorious gods we see,
We learn from everything our fancies teach.
   Yet in the infinity of mind we feel
   The solid wall that circles what is real.

At Pendle Hill

SONNET FOR NAILS

14 January 1992

Carpenter of the Spirit, hammer your nails
Into the wooden fragments of my mind,
And craft, from all the models Heaven designed,
The furniture of crosses, altars, grails.
I learn not from the scholars, but from tales
Told by plain folk, caught in the earthly grind
Of toil and poverty, who strangely find
Unlikely heavenly winds that fill their sails.

They talked about what they had seen and heard,
'Til journalists named Mark, Matthew, and Luke
Wrote the good gossip down, and Gospels took
On the bright aura of a Book and Word.
    O Carpenter, they nailed you to the wood,
    Not knowing nails turn into seeds of good.

FOR THE CHRIST WITHIN
Spring 1988

O, Christ within, run thy anointed power
Through all the trampled mazes of my mind,
Open the way to what I cannot find,
And close the paths where love and hope turn sour.
Invade my castle with its glassy tower
From whence I look, powerless, on human kind
And with the gentle cords of love fast bind
Me to the one, shining, eternal hour.

And then? And then? Always there is "And then?"
After redemption, what? Is there a brink
Beyond which line there is no time to think,
Because there is no time, no now, no when.
    Nothing to laugh with, nothing to appall,
    For everything is timeless, spaceless, All.

AT THE CHAPEL, ATLANTA AIRPORT
30 December 1989

Dare I indeed call you not "Lord," but "Friend"?*
Creator of all creation: the unfriendly, vast,
Blind universe, stretching from endless past
To futures with unimaginable end.
Could a conceivable Creator send
To earth's small speck of dust, at last,
The image of a Friend, to cast
Its healing shade, to lift, to bless, to mend?

In time, only the probable takes place;
But gaze upon the infinite, and see
The happening of improbability,
The glorious unlikelihood of grace.
    So in the smallest part of space and time,
    Friendship alone blazes with light Divine.

(*cf. John 15:15)

SONNET FOR THE GREAT PROPHETS

31 May 1992

I must confess I do not understand
What gives great prophets their enormous power
To change the world, with spiritual dower
Passed on through time by some devoted band,
Helped by some holy writ kept close at hand.
When threats try to make unbelievers cower,
The prophet's message turns a little sour,
But then, for Reformation there's demand.

They come, roughly five hundred years apart:
Moses, Confucius, Buddha, Jesus—then
Mohammed, Luther. Who knows where or when
The next will come to bring a change of heart?
    Now that we have one world, fearful of doom,
    For a great prophet there is surely room.

SONNET FOR BUDDHISM
6 April 1992

In the long night of human suffering
A mountain prince once caught a sliver of dawn;
That uncontrolled desire would surely spawn
Life after life, the pain that life would bring.
And so, not wanting to become a king
In inner contemplation was withdrawn;
Not wanting either to become a pawn
He achieved peace—a strange and precious thing.

Yet out of this came love: the eightfold way
Of sheer compassion for all living kind;
Precursor of the teaching from the mind
Of One who was five hundred years away.
    And so Detachment, under Love transformed,
    Makes multitudes of hearts so strangely warmed!

AT L'ABBAYE DE ROYAUMONT

15 December 1985, 2 a.m.

Now in the middle of the winter night
The great church rises in my wakeful mind.
In the gray light of day, all I can find
Are low foundations less than human height;
But dark, and restlessness, suddenly ignite
Imagination, to throw up the blind
That shields us from the past. The old monks lined
Once more the choir in all its Gothic might,

Chants and dim candles fill dark sacred space,
The mass is said, bodies to pallets go.
Imagined time speeds its remorseless flow
And brings me to the present time and place
    Whatever was, still is, in all minds deep
    And now in peace I can return to sleep.

AT 3:00 A.M. FOR RIGHT AND LEFT
12 January 1992

To walk or run★ we must have two good feet.
No bird can fly unless it has two wings.
To mount as eagles, as the prophet sings,
Two separate powers must in the body meet.
One mouth is all we need to have to eat,
One heart, one brain to all the body brings
The life through which one throat joyfully sings
The song that makes the diverse parts complete.

How can we solve this endless paradox?
The love that turns two into one makes three,
And keeps both separateness and unity.
With right and left wings birds can fly in flocks.
    Victory of one can't put an end to strife;
    'Tis love alone that brings continuous life.

(★cf. Isaiah 40:31)

SONNET FOR "FILIOQUE"*

18 March 1992

How can it be that just a single word
Within a creed should split the Christian Church
For bitter centuries? Yet we need to search
For meaning, even in what seems absurd,
For words, like flags, can madden us to gird
Ourselves for war, while leaving in the lurch
The bonds that bind us to the fragile perch
Where the soft tones of love and peace are heard.

Then should the Holy Spirit's power proceed
Only from the Father, as the East declares,
Or from the Son as well, as the West dares
To say, emblazoned in its Latin creed?—
    Perhaps making a very subtle sign
    That God is human, as well as Divine.

*(*Filioque—"and the son"—was added to the Nicene Greed by the Western
church in the eighth century. The version in the Episcopal Book of Common
Prayer reads, "I believe in the Holy Ghost, the Lord and Giver of Life, who
proceedeth from the Father and the Son.")*

SONNET FOR BAPTISM

5 September 1986

Yes, water washes, cleanses, purifies;
There's nothing like an early morning swim
Toward the splendor of earth's eastern rim
To cleanse both mind and skin, where'er dirt lies.
But holy fire can deeper far baptize
Consuming rage, hate, lust; and grief can dim
The inward flames, and from their ashes grim
The Phoenix of our spirit can arise.

But greatest is the baptism of light,
From light we came, to light we shall return,
What's washed will soil, what's burned again will burn.
But shadows serve to show what is in sight,
    And in the ocean of pure light and love,
      There's no east, west; here, there; below, above.

Found and revised, 12 January 1992

SONNET FOR MATTER
15 January 1992

Beyond the narrow wall of time and space
My soul leaps out toward infinitude,
Perhaps by curiosity pursued
Or drawn by faint and distant songs of grace.
But Body stays in its accustomed place,
Surrounded by chairs, tables, cupboards, food,
Trees, mountains, skies—an earthly multitude
Of matter—that both good and bad include.

Spirit is the Creator. Lowly matter
Is what's created. But Creation's word
Needs energy and matter to be heard
In gene, voice, print, brain, even in chatter.
    Matter to spirit is a younger brother;
    Neither can prosper well without the other.

SONNET FOR INFINITY
13 June 1986

Seldom have I beheld such cloudless sky,
A hemisphere of blue without one spot.
The night sky's specked with stars, but this is not;
I cannot see where any limits lie.
It is the one occasion when the eye
Can see infinity. No why or what
Troubles the seeing mind. The eye-beams shot
Beyond the horizon reach no boundary.

And this infinity of blue is One.
My resonating mind feels strangely kin
With ancient patriarchs who dwelt within
The desert lands, and learned firmly to shun
    The pantheons of imagined deities,
    And saw One God, to rule infinities.

Ghost Ranch, New Mexico

ON MARRIAGE AND HOME

SONNET FOR MY WIFE ELISE ON THE OCCASION OF HER SEVENTIETH BIRTHDAY,

6 July 1990

Seventy is a kind of magic number,
When life, for some, is thought to reach its peak;
For others, like yourself, it's a mystique
That merely lifts the shackles that encumber
Our earlier years, that tie to us useless lumber,
Obscuring what we really need to seek.
It is a vision, and a call to speak
Of new awakenings, and not of slumber.

To this I testify! My seventies
Have been the richest decade of my life,
And I am sure that you, beloved wife,
Will find the same sweet freedom in the breeze
    That has upheld our wings these precious years
    And brought amazing joy beyond tears.

SONNET FOR THE GOLDEN WEDDING OF KENNETH AND ELISE BOULDING,
31 August 1991
4 June 1991

My mind swings back to that first day we met,
When Love's clear holy light flared up between us.
After that meeting, nothing could demean us,
And after fifty years it's shining yet.
Then Love committed, bravely did beget
A wondrous tribe—something poor shell-bound Venus
Could not achieve, til You-I came to mean Us,
Beyond the reach of life's turmoil and fret.

So have we lived upon a rich plateau;
True, life together is not without its cliffs—
Misunderstandings, separations, tiffs
Can slope toward a precipice below,
 But love, true love, always turned us around,
 And here we stand, still on love's holy ground.

(in bed)

SONNET FOR BELATED REVELATION
5 July 1992

Once, with my good wife at a conference,
I was defined and treated as a spouse
And urged to be quiet as a mouse
Even though what I might have said made sense.
I will confess I found myself quite tense
At being such an outcast in the house
Not even being invited to carouse,
But pushed behind a quite exclusive fence.

And then it hit me like a blaze of light
That this was how my wife was treated many times.
I had never thought of this as crimes
Against the fundamental right
    Of personal identity. My wife
    Has suffered this in silence all her life.

SONNET FOR MY WIFE'S ABSENCE
21 March 1992

The house is silent when you are away
Unnaturally so! I still sing hymns
While I am washing dishes, stretch my limbs
With little chants when in my bath I stay
At the beginning of the long, long day.
But I am restless, polishing the rims
Of spectacles, as my eye quickly skims
The morning paper by my breakfast tray.

Even the telephone has ceased to ring,
For people know that you are not in town.
Outside, the quiet snow is drifting down,
And silence is enfolding everything,
    And as on our half-empty bed I lie,
    My mind is waiting for your entering cry.

SONNET FOR ORDINARY DAILY LIFE

19 November 1992

Now let me sing the unaffected praise
Of simple, ordinary daily life—
The blessings of a long-devoted wife,
The constant rhythm of domestic days.
Poets have sung too many sumptuous lays
To the sad histories of public strife,
The wars and battles that are much too rife
But pass. It is domestic life that stays!

The learning that goes on outside the schools
From parents and grandparents of the young
And gives mute babes a common mind and tongue,
This is what gives us all the subtle tools
 That craft us into bodies with a mind
 Each with a mysterious self assigned.

SONNET FOR COMING HOME
16 February 1992

Let me sing praises to familiar things
That punctuate the dailyness of life,
Free from excitement, novelty, and strife;
Bed, breakfast, dinner, lunch, old wedding rings,
The daily paper that the morning brings,
The cup and saucer, spoon and fork and knife,
And most of all, my long-beloved wife.
Outside, a squirrel jumps, a small bird sings.

I have indeed adventured round this earth
Of which I count myself a citizen;
I love its vast variety, but when
I travel home again, the precious worth,
    The endless wonder of the commonplace
    Fills up my smiling soul with joy and grace.

SONNET FOR OUR HUMBLE HOME
24 July 1992

"Humble" perhaps is not the proper word.
I'm proud it speaks our creativity
For we helped to design it, carefully
Probing perfection as not quite absurd
So every little detail we referred
To the great test: Would it make our lives free?
This we accomplished quite successfully,
And if we had been cats we would have purred!

The bedroom has convenience close at hand,
The kitchen looks out to the dancing trees,
Across the dining room, to where one sees
The living quarters comfortably planned.
    Beyond, a balcony with mountain views
    Within, two studies, each for one to use.

WAKING AT DAWN
23 November 1992

The snow-filled cloud is now but yards away
And my horizon is the next door roof.
Even the nearest neighbor seems aloof.
The one red chimney pokes above the gray.
It looks as if it's going to snow all day,
It feels as though the whole world has gone "poof."
Yet of existence I now have the proof—
My lovely wife brings in the breakfast tray!

And soon I will get up and put on clothes
And wrap my eyes around a science book
That opens to my mind a vast new nook
Where precious human understanding grows,
 And the vast complex world in which we live
 Is spread before us in the mind's bright sieve.

SONNET FOR MY MORNING TUB
12 March 1992

What pearls of wisdom can a bathtub hold;
Is it not daily, commonplace, and trite?
Ah well! Immersion is a sacred rite
Of spiritual power, so I've been told.
If water is too hot, turn on the cold;
If it's too cold, the hot tap makes it right.
The Aristotelian Mean's clearly in sight
And in our power! How wisdom can unfold!

And then, of course, the soap will make me clean,
The shower will wash off vestiges of soap,
So, in the morning ritual, signs of hope
For a whole world of cleansing I can glean.
    The water grunts as it goes down the drain,
    "O.K.—tomorrow you'll be in again."

SONNET FOR GETTING TO SLEEP
17-18 May 1992

After I get to bed I like to read
A little, to calm down my wandering mind;
Then I turn off the light, only to find
A Universe expand beyond my need;
A planet gazes on me, like a bead
Of steady light, far, far, from humankind;
Stars twinkle, and I find myself resigned
To be from sleep a short while to be freed.

I see myself a minute molecule
In the vast reaches of the universe,
And yet within me strange, vast fancies nurse
Infinities—maybe myself to fool.
    And then I shut my eyes. I'm home again,
    And sleep covers me in my cozy den.

ON TIME

SONNET FOR TIME
October 1988

As a small eddy in the stream of time
I cannot much affect its mighty course,
Yet this reflection leads not to remorse,
For I can spin and dance to rhythm and rhyme,
And though the water may be streaked with grime
And moves with seeming unrelentless force,
It springs up clear from many a holy source,
And purifies itself of sludge and slime.

A thick mist hangs over the stream ahead.
Do I hear thunder of a waterfall?
Out of the stream I am not powered to crawl,
But as I dance, some energy is fed
    Into the stream, to make it understand
    Its destination is a promised land.

SONNET FOR A CALENDAR

6 February 1993

Rich and relentless as a music box,
My memory will not wholly let me go,
Although the product is not much to show
Beyond the childlike charm of building blocks.
Still, there are times when fleeting memory locks
Itself into a pattern and a flow
Out of which meaning, with a radiant glow,
Can suddenly make sense of patterned clocks.

All structures fall, but when they fall in place
With older ranks of time, they make good sense—
Two follows one; three, two; four, three, without pretense.
Then, suddenly, a calendar we sense;
    Days, weeks, months, seasons, years, are safely mated
    And time, above all else, is celebrated.

SONNET FOR CHANGE

15 January 1992

What laws can govern unexpected change?
How does the New emerge from out the Old?
Not even alchemists turned dross to gold.
All transformations lie within a range.
How, then, does the familiar become strange?
How do tales spread that never have been told,
Great buttresses collapse that should uphold,
And booms and busts bedevil the Exchange?

These are the greatest mysteries of the mind;
We grope toward the future in a mist,
The best that we can do is make a list
Of future good and bad that we can find.
    How to survive? Expect the unexpected,
    And correct fast what needs to be corrected.

SONNET FOR CYCLES

22 February 1992

Cycles surround us, soon as we come to be;
Wake-sleep, wake-sleep, night-day, dark-light, night-day;
Feeding at intervals pursues its way,
The moon's never from monthly patterns free.
Seasons follow each other relentlessly,
And, as we grow under new learning's sway,
Planets in big and little circles play.
For some, each day at four o'clock brings tea.

Birds flap their wings and migrate forth and back.
Yet still I do believe time has an arrow.
Great Cycles?—No!—they make the mind too narrow,
For Evolution follows an upward track
    Which my small self can climb as knowledge grows
    From God's Creation. To what end? Who knows?

THE LOS ANGELES AIRPORT, FROM THE RED CARPET CLUB

6 February 1992

The sky, the grounds, the buildings, all are gray;
Only the standing planes show red and blue.
The groundsmen in the rain, a motley crew
In black and yellow garb, put bags away
Into a plane; wet, on a rainy day.
Pools on the ground reflect a darker hue,
Drops on the window pane obscure the view,
A plane sears into the clouds with no delay.

And I am waiting in a slice of time,
Cut out between arriving and departing,
A respite from the business of carting
Body and bags around. It's not sublime!
    But suddenly a thought drops into me—
    In time, emptiness is not vacancy.

FROM EARLHAM
February 1990

Each of us is a leaf, high on a tree.
The sap that makes us grow comes from a ground
We cannot even see. The air around
That we must breathe, blows, carelessly and free,
From elsewhere. Of the world's great symphony
All we can hear is but a rustling sound.
Yet we feel part of something more profound,
And you are not just you, nor I just me.

The busy passing decades of our lives
Are but a brief flash in eternity.
If our leaf had not sprouted, would the tree
Have noticed it, as it still grows and thrives?
    And yet—and yet—the greatest tree can't live
    Without the nurture that the small leaves give.

SONNET FOR MAINTENANCE
24 April 1992

Time is a nibbler, and all things decay,
Mountains erode, and rivers fill with silt,
And every temple humankind has built
Crumbles. Our precious bodies turn to clay,
All colors fade and turn into a gray,
And every lovely flower is doomed to wilt,
Edifices of pride crack into guilt,
Garbage accumulates and garments fray.

So let us always give unstinting praise
To those who heal the endless wounds of time,
Brave souls who deal with garbage and with grime,
And fix and mend and heal in many ways.
    Always to make new things makes little sense
    If we neglect the work of maintenance.

ON AGING, SICKNESS, AND DYING

SONNET FOR AGING
12-13 April 1992

Too close to the last chapter of my life
I feel a fear of what it may be like,
For they are fortunate whom death can strike
With a sharp, swift, and almost painless knife.
Uncertain fears around my mind are rife,
Who wants a long, boring, and crippled hike
Across mud flats, surrounded by a dike
That hides the great ocean of joy and strife?

Enough! I share the lot of humankind,
What lies beyond the end I do not know;
If nothing, then it's better far to go
Into the void than live with half a mind.
    If something, then I see no need to fear,
    For what has been far, then may become near.

SONNET FOR MY LIFE'S PLATEAU
7-8 June 1992

My life has been lived on a broad plateau,
Feeling, I know not how, strangely secure.
The spiritual air is very pure.
But at the edge I sense a world below
Of war, pain, fear, and endless human woe.
I offer only sympathy, not cure;
I mouth only the bitter word "Endure";
You cannot get to where you cannot go.

And so I wait. Not too far from the cliff.
Hearing the sounds that from below me rise
I hope—for what? For some unknown surprise
That will transform the ever-threatening "if."
    One does not have to be an adventist
    To put some second comings on our list!

SONNET FOR OLD AGE
23 June 1992

Surely no road goes downhill all the way;
One finds all sorts of "ups" among the "downs,"
Patches of color interrupt the browns,
And brighter lights will shine among the gray.
A "yes" will often follow after "nay,"
As pleasant inns are found in ugly towns,
Exciting verbs come after the dull nouns,
And lovely pots emerge from ugly clay.

Sickness is ended by renewing health,
Old age has treasures youth cannot achieve,
With freedom from demands, and time to spare
Relaxing in a comfortable chair;
Then when the time comes with its call to leave,
    To join the historic past of humankind,
      Gently we can depart with peace of mind.

SONNET FOR MEMORY
3 January 1993

Precious beyond all price is memory,
Without which mind's a prisoner of the hour,
Losing its blessedly unconscious power
To expand the present toward eternity
Of past, and even future, that we see
As a vast complicated tower
Stretching up to the future clouds that lower
And reaching down into geology!

And now, in old age, memory grows dim
Of yesterday, though not of yesteryear.
Of the more distant past the view is clear,
The nearer past becomes a fuzzy rim.
 Still, records, notes can partly take its place,
 For memory never dies without a trace.

SONNET FOR PHYSICAL ENERGY
30 May 1992

In terms of calories, the food I eat
Is much the same as what I did when young.
The oxygen I take into my lung
With breath has had a very constant beat.
But when it comes to energy, my feet
Move very slowly, though my gabbling tongue
Still chatters, and the ideas that have sprung
From out my mind still don't show much retreat.

Physical energy seems to fade with age,
For what goes in does not seem to come out;
But information has the skill to flout
The conservation laws. Brain cells engage
   Themselves with very little energy;
   Muscles may lag, but Muse keeps up her spree!

SONNET FOR MY MUSE

Written as I was going off to sleep after reading sonnets
19 January 1992

The fires that drove me once are burning lower;
The energies that earlier would drive
The missile of my body, still may thrive
But at a pace distinguishably slower.
My inner Muse—Ah, me! how much I owe her—
Still shows no signs of failure to survive,
And manages to be so much alive
That she knows me much better than I know her!

So let it be! What if the striding pace
At which my long life has been lived must slow—
Still, there are places where I have to go,
And have the time to crawl rather than race.
    And it's not I that's slow—Old Time, my master,
    Decided he can move a little faster!

REFLECTIONS INSPIRED BY
SHAKESPEARE'S SONNETS
16 April 1985

Now have I spots on my once spotless skin,
My once-jet hair is now a spotless white.
I am no longer potent in the night,
And softer grows the world's incessant din.
But when I turn my still sharp gaze within,
Great landscapes of the past blaze into light,
And even if some scenes slip out of sight,
Yet every day new scenes to view come in.

So, Time, be not too proud; even decay
Makes ruins still more lovely. My mind's eye
Shall see increasing spaces till I die,
And, even then, who knows what powers may sway
    The kingdoms of my mind; what crystal pool
    May then reflect the Universe, as jewel?

SONNET FOR MY STIFF KNEES
29 December 1991

The human body is a work of art,
Sketched by its genes, and painted by its brain;
It heals itself, again and then again,
Its whole is healed by many a different part.
It's like a horse, too, pulling a complex cart
But sometimes, traveling in a rough domain,
The parts rebel, and though with might and main
The horse pulls, still the wheels refuse to start.

But brain's unique. It can call other brains
And bodies too, to operate, to feed,
To dose, to exercise the parts in need
Until their health returns, and long remains.
    So knees, I thank you for your gifts to me,
    And later, both of you may thankful be.

SONNET FOR SLEEPLESSNESS
22 March 1992

My legs can't seem to find a place to rest,
The thoughts that throng my mind randomly creep,
Make no good sense, deprive me of my sleep,
And seem to wander on a useless quest.
My stomach whines that it must still digest
My supper, sheets and blankets in a heap
Refuse to disentangle. Counting sheep
Gets nowhere. It's too early to get dressed.

And then—how strange—it is already morning.
The gray light of the sky outlines the hills.
Dim in my memory are the past night's ills.
I am awake—a new day is a-borning,
    And all the subtle terrors of the night
    Retreat and vanish in the morning light.

SONNET FOR MY BODY AND MIND
10 April 1992

I

I'm grateful for my body—but to whom?
The slightly tarnished mantle of my skin
Encloses a cell-universe within,
Somehow including the enormous room
Of consciousness, extending into gloom,
Lit by a flashlight, that can gather in
Patterns of worlds, at least somewhat akin
To the real worlds of truth that round me loom.

But then, in all this vastness, who am I?
A ruler?—sometimes ruling, sometimes not,
When accidents, diseases, sins have got
Control, and roughly pass me by?
    To one great question answers none I find:
    How can a body be home to a mind?

SONNET FOR MY BODY AND MIND
10 April 1992

II

My mind is like a huge department store.
Filled with the memories of eighty years
I walk the aisles, go up and down the stairs,
From where I am now on the topmost floor,
Past times and places where I've lived before,
People I knew, books, hopes, thoughts, joys, and cares,
The vast variety that memory bears.
Then constantly I pass a blank, closed door

Behind which lie great stores of things forgot.
And somewhere lying in this vast domain
I find an imperfect image of my brain,
Billions of neurons in a tangled knot.
  Yet in the image of my brain I find
  Nothing that's like the content of my mind!

SONNET FOR SICKNESS
17 June 1992

It is a strange exhaustion that I feel;
The limits of my energy close in,
Feeling almost as near me as my skin.
The outside world seems suddenly unreal,
I find I cannot adequately deal
With small frustrations. Then, I lift my chin
And force my moping mouth into a grin,
I find myself on a more even keel.

Then, if I can relax my muscles tense
And lie down for a little while,
The empty grin becomes a cheerful smile
And suddenly the world starts making sense.
    If chemistry perhaps can cure this ill,
    I'll ask my doctor for another pill!

SONNET FOR PAIN

1 March 1992

Pain is a signal that there's something wrong,
A red light on the dashboard of the brain,
A frowning teacher with a threatening cane,
A buzzing fire alarm, a warning gong.
A sign of something that does not belong,
A signal that there's loss rather than gain,
It is not to be treated with disdain
Or turned away from when it goes "ding-dong."

And yet it seems to be so overdone,
An agony, when all we need's an itch.
Worse, pain of spirit fails to tell us which
Dragon it is from which we ought to run.
　　So, when we want a curing to be quick
　　It's best to use the carrot, not the stick.

SONNET FOR A PILL

12-13 April 1992

How strange the body is when it gets ill.
A little falter of some chemical
Can strike the nerves with pain inimical
To comfort or to sleep or peace, until
The doctor can prescribe a little pill
That chases pain away—so magical
That one is tempted to be cynical
And think the cure lies only in the will!

Magic or chemistry—I don't much care.
I'm only glad that some solutions dance
On the great ocean of our ignorance,
And that a cure can sometimes be found there.
    But still, I seem to sense an inner need
    To know why some cures fail and some succeed.

SONNET FOR HANDICAPS
24 June 1992

Faced with increasing stiffness of the knees
I join the country of the handicapped,
A realm I must confess I never mapped
And saw it somehow as far overseas.
Now to its gates I find I have the keys
And to its culture I must now adapt.
I must confess I feel a little trapped,
For in this world I don't feel quite at ease.

Nevertheless, this world has courtesy
Far beyond what the normal world can find.
Wheelchairs and walking sticks seem well designed
To call forth help, and smiles, and sympathy.
    It is perhaps the handicapped who see
    Humans as a productive family.

SONNET FOR CORRUPTION
8 April 1992

Corruption is a universal law;
The lithest body ages, stiffens, dies,
And it should come to us as no surprise
To find that every system has a flaw.
The luscious food we cram into our maw
Turns into excrement. Words that are wise
Become a folly. Truth turns into lies.
Nothing's exempt from time's relentless claw.

Is there a Second Law of Everything,
That once potential's realized it's gone,
And the rich world of life we look upon
Is nothing but a temporary fling?
    Death and Corruption's what we pay for birth;
    But oh! let's not pay more than it is worth!

OUTRAGEOUS JOY

24 January 1993

Joy is outrageous. Here we are on a cliff
In a cloud; and we know there is a brink
That well may be much closer than we think,
We could be over it in just a jiff.
Over all broods the silent sound of "if"
And even where we stand we sense a stink
Of pain and human misery—we shrink
And then comes, almost like a clown saying "Piff,"

Absurd joy to the world, the Lord is come
Like fresh sap rising in a withered tree
A flame of praise, rising exultantly
Beyond all reason in a world so glum.
    There is a vast refreshment in the sky—
    What matters cliffs indeed to those who fly!

ON HEARING OF A SUDDEN DEATH
29 January 1983

Lord, Lord, is it thy messenger who knocks?
A rap, re-echoing through my cheerful room,
The windows shadowed by a sudden gloom,
Silence descending on the ticking clocks.
My sweating hands cannot unbolt the locks,
My frozen, quivering knees seem to assume
That all that lies outside the door is doom,
And my unwilling mind sets up new blocks.

Hope's candle sputters, and Faith's lamp burns low.
Does then the darkness hide only more dark?
Does the door open only on the stark
Vast emptiness of naught—no bliss, no woe?
   Only love, steadfast, stays. That light is steady,
   And when the door flings wide, I will be ready.

Orlando, Florida
Written in memory of Byron T. Conrad, South Eastern Yearly Meeting Treasurer (d. 22 January 1983).

SONNET FOR DEATH
7 November 1992

Death is an experience every living thing,
Given enough time, will experience once
And only once. Who would be such a dunce
As to ask for repetition? Life can bring
Breakfast, lunch, tea, and dinner in a string
Of almost equal intervals whose runs
May be repeated in a string (by some)
Making a spiral rather than a ring.

Small deaths of course we can experience.
New schools, new jobs, new houses—even new wives—
Can dot the temporal pattern of our lives.
We can revisit in the present tense,
And yet to all of us old time will send
The greatest of events that marks . . . The End!